War Diary

THE GERMAN LIST

War Diary

INGEBORG BACHMANN

WITH LETTERS FROM JACK HAMESH

EDITED, WITH AN AFTERWORD, BY HANS HÖLLER

TRANSLATED BY MIKE MITCHELL

LONDON NEW YORK CALCUTTA

GOETHE-INSTITUT

This publication was supported by a grant
from the Goethe-Institut India

Seagull Books, 2011

Kriegstagebuch
Mit Briefen von Jack Hamesh an Ingeborg Bachmann

Edited, with an afterword, by Hans Höller
© Suhrkamp Verlag, Berlin 2010

First published in English by Seagull Books, 2011
English translation © Mike Mitchell, 2011

ISBN-13   978 0 8574 2 008 4

Typeset and designed by Seagull Books, Calcutta, India
Printed and bound by Hyam Enterprises, Calcutta, India

CONTENTS

ACKNOWLEDGEMENTS

I would like to express my thanks to the following persons and institutions who were involved in the search for Jack Hamesh:

Evelyn Adunka (historian, Vienna), Ada Brodsky (translator, Israel), Odell David (The Douglas E. Goldman Jewish Genealogy Center, Israel), Malkitta Dubnikov (Irgun-Jeckes), Howard Falksohn (The Wiener Library, London), Wolf-Erich Eckstein (Israelitische Kultusgemeinde, Vienna), Abraham Frank (Irgun Olej Merkas Europa, Ramat Gan), Haim Ghiuzeli (Databases Department, Beit Hatfutsot, Tel Aviv), Andrea Goodmaker (Association of Jewish Refugees, UK), Devorah Haberfeld (Irgun Yozei Merkaz Europa, Israel), Rosemary Hoffmann (Jewish Genealogical Society of Great Britain), Briony Kay (National Archives of the United Kingdom), Elisabeth Klamper (Dokumentationsarchiv des Österreichischen Widerstands, Vienna), Debbie Korenstein (Global Center for Israel), Lilian Levy (World Jewish Relief, United Kingdom), Micha Limor (editor of the information newsletter of MB Yakinton), Mark Lowen (British Foreign and Commonwealth

Office), Reuven Merhav (Irgun Yozei Merkaz Europa, Israel), Derek Montgomery (Service Personnel and Veteran's Agency, UK), Michaela Laichmann, Ferdinand Opll, Manuel Swatek (Stadt- und Landesarchiv, Vienna), Christine Horwitz (Magistrat der Stadt Wien), Irene Sullivan (The National Archives of Australia), Christine Tropper (Kärntner Landesarchiv), Yad Vashem Holocaust Martyrs' and Heroes' Remembrance Authority.

I would like to thank the following for their great readiness to help and support me in my editorial work:

Ingeborg Bachmann's brother and sister: Isolde Moser (Kötschach) and Heinz Bachmann (Abingdon and Bratislava), Anne Betten (University of Salzburg), Armin Eidherr (Zentrum für Jüdische Kultur an der Universität Salzburg), Marina Jamritsch (teacher at the Gymnasium in Hermagor), Mike Lyons (translator, Abingdon, served with the FSS in Carinthia), Doron Rabinovici (writer, Vienna), Erich Stöller (psychoanalyst, Salzburg), Wilheldm Wadl (Kärntner Landesarchiv), and, last but not least, my wife Ulrike for organizing and administering the research.

Hans Höller

WAR DIARY

Dear Diary, now I'm saved. I don't have to go to Poland, nor to bazooka training. Papa was here in Vellach[1] and went to Klagenfurt; he went to see Dr Hasler, who advised him to register me for the teacher-training college immediately, since so many teachers are needed. Not in my wildest dreams would I have thought the day would come when the hated teacher-training college would be my salvation. I was accepted immediately and enrolled in the final-year class, actually for a crash course and you have to teach while you're still at the college. Everything went smoothly at the district offices. The only unpleasant part was with the woman responsible for female students liable for substitute service.[2] I went twice, the first time she wasn't there, I could hardly remember her, her face, only the terrible registration at which she told me I had to 'behave myself' otherwise I would be

for it despite my good report. And the way she said
'girl' with a triple 'i'. This time she wanted to give
me a good talking-to again but I forestalled her
because I knew how you had to go about it from
H. and I told her that now I was quite sure I was
unsuited to university and therefore wanted to be a
teacher, also because it was more important for the
war effort, for the children, I added, and there was
nothing she could object to in that. The only problem was that I knew that you had to sign a form
with a legally binding declaration that you relin-
quished your right to attend university. I hesitated
for a moment and then signed. No, I'm sure I won't
go to university, not in this country, not during this
war. Crazy to hesitate even for a moment. Today
was the first lesson. I was almost glad to be sitting
in a classroom again. But can you call it a classroom? I think all the girls in the class are fanatics.
After the first lesson there was an air-raid alarm
and that was that. But Wilma from our year at
school is there too. She did the same as me. She
didn't come with me but went home to Annabichl
on her bicycle, and I'm lying here in our favourite
spot, on the edge of the woods. Issi[3] has brought the
meal pap from the chemist's again and we mix it

with water from the stream. Sunshine. She's sleeping and sunbathing, the alarm has lasted five hours already. Still no bombs. At one point there were two low-flying aircraft and they let off a few rounds.

The Russians are in Vienna and probably already somewhere in Styria as well. I've discussed everything with Issi. It's not that easy. She doesn't know whether or not she can get something out of the poison cabinet. We're both afraid of the Russians. I refuse to believe everything people say but no one can foresee what they'll do with us, whether they'll leave us here or take us to Siberia. By now we have to expect the worst.

What will you do, God, if I die . . . [4] I don't go up to the air-raid shelter any more. The Tschörners are already dead and Ali went the next day. Our Ali.[5] There's no one left in our street any more. The days are so sunny. I've taken a chair out to the garden and I'm reading. I have firmly resolved to carry on reading when the bombs come. The *Stundenbuch* is already creased and smudged. It's my only comfort. And Baudelaire! Bientot nous tomberons dans les froides tenebres, adieu vive clarte. I don't need to look at the book any more. Yesterday, the biggest formation we've ever had came. The first flew on, the second dropped its bombs. The roar was so deafening I couldn't breathe and I went down into the cellar after all, which is actually ridiculous in our little house since it wouldn't even stand up to a little bomb, never mind a 100 kg bomb. They say things look terrible in the town and even out here it looks like the end of the world. I'm not afraid any more, only a physical feeling when the bombs drop, something clenches up inside me. But in my mind I've made my will. Perhaps it's sinful just to sit and look at the sun. But I can't go back down in the shelter any more, for hours, with the water running down the walls, and it gets so stuffy it almost makes you faint. You're not allowed to talk because of the air but still the dull, mute masses in there are unbearable. I find the idea of perhaps perishing down there with the lot of them, like a herd of cattle, horrifying. At least in the garden. At least in the sunshine.

This morning Anderluh said we weren't to leave the college when there's a full-scale alarm any more. He's behaving like a madman. Early on, he saw Wilma wearing her silver chain with the cross and was so furious he almost threw her down the stairs. At 7 o'clock tomorrow morning we all have to go to the fields outside Annabichl to dig trenches, 'Klagenfurt has to be defended to the last man and the last woman', he bellowed. Straight away I discussed what to do with Wilma. She can't go, she has to look after her brothers and sisters. They've been bombed out and her's mother's in hospital somewhere, seriously ill. I'll go myself and check out the situation, if necessary I'll think up some excuse for her. But Issi, dear old Issi, comforted me, we went to the edge of the woods again, and eventually we were even laughing. The 'man taking cover' was there again, crawling around twenty metres away from us like a startled weasel. When the low-flying planes strafed the trains, he kept popping his head up out of the bushes and shouting hysterically, 'Cover, ladies! Take cover, ladies!'—and Issi, who nearly chokes once she really starts laughing, ended up gasping for breath and saying, 'My, isn't he well brought up!' Then she told me the latest jokes she's heard from their chemist's shop and we ate cold potatoes. I'll need to be on my toes tomorrow.

All the children were there for the digging but not a single teacher, not even Anderluh, needless to say. Naturally, the form prefects were in charge

and, anyway, no one in the whole flock of sheep
had any idea of the arrogance of these teachers,
our supposed role models. I was so furious I just
poked about in the hard ground with my spade a
bit, I didn't feel sick at all but I must have gone all
white because after half an hour the girl next to
me said, 'Do you feel sick?' I muttered something
vague, all the time I was just thinking: It's outra-
geous what they're doing to us. These grown-ups,
these high-and-mighty 'educators', who want to let
us get killed. When the full-scale alarm came, a
couple of the smaller ones started to get a bit agi-
tated, no house and no cellar for miles around, and
the factories nearby! Nearby was a wooden hut and
a bombed-out market garden. My bike was there
and I said I needed to sit down for a moment.
Unfortunately for me, just before that a few of the
older leaders from the Hitler Youth had come to
check the trenches and they shouted 'Carry on'.
Despite that I left, I leant against the side of the hut
and, as no one could see me very well, I jumped on
my bike and rode off. The bombs were already
falling when I reached Pischeldorferstrasse, I lay in
an old crater in the meadow and rode on half an
hour later, to Wilma's.

Wilma seems to have calmed down. Neither of us is going to go to the college any more. Not all the teachers know us, anyway. Anderluh probably doesn't know me at all and Hasler certainly won't say anything. Wilma's afraid we might be shot for desertion but in the confusion there is at the moment I think there's absolutely no likelihood anyone will bother with us. I've got the most important things together in the cellar. When the time comes, I'm going to take them with me to the Gail valley. But for the moment, I'm staying here. I found Liselotte in a box. I put the frilly pink dress on her and now she's lying in bed with me. She can't say 'Mama' any more, nor can I. Oh, Mummy, Mummy! And Heinerle,[6] my angel! No post. Nothing.

No, there's no point in talking to grown-ups any more.

Everyone living within ten kilometres of the border needs an identity card. Vellach is still in the border zone. If you want an identity card or are looking for work, you have to go to the FSS.[7] I don't know what that means, some say Secret Service but of course that's nonsense. I went there today and didn't have to wait long to be seen. There were two Englishmen in the office, one very wild-looking, with a beard, they say he's from South Africa; the other's short and on the ugly side, glasses, speaks fluent German with a Viennese accent. The South African doesn't speak it so well, just broken German. The little one got me to fill out the forms, then he looked at me and said, 'Aha, you've taken your Matura.'[8] I imagine he was surprised because all the other girls are peasant girls. Then he said, 'BdM,[9] of course.' I suddenly felt quite sick and didn't utter a word, just nodded. Of course I could have told him that I probably wasn't on any lists any longer, as I didn't transfer at fourteen and was never sworn in either, and that after that I was never roped in for meetings nor went to any. But I don't know what was the matter with me. Also, I thought that everyone probably told him that they weren't members and that they'd only been forced to go, and I immediately assumed he wouldn't believe a word of what I said. Finally he said: 'Think again carefully whether you were a leader. We'll find out if you were.' I managed to stammer, 'No'. But I think I blushed bright red and I was so desperate I went even redder. I simply can't understand why you blush and tremble when you're telling the truth.

Yesterday I went to enquire about my identity card. Only the South African was there; it'll be a few days before I get my card. By the greengrocer's, below the District Council offices, the other one suddenly got off his bicycle. He could still remember my name and was quite different, not mocking any more, embarrassed if anything. He's called Jack Hamesh. I was quite embarrassed too. He asked me where I lived in Vellach and walked with me as far as the bridge. I don't know why he wanted to talk to me. He asked whether Uncle Christl is related to me and of course I said yes, adding that almost everyone called B. is related to us. Why Uncle Christl was sent to a camp when the G.s and M.s were the most fanatical Nazis of all, I don't know; everybody thinks the G.s are behind it, they were always our rivals in the village and now, anyway, everyone's denouncing everyone else, especially the Nazis are denouncing each other because they all think that way they can get off themselves. Of course, I didn't say a word of what I was thinking, I'm sure he wouldn't have understood and, after all, I hardly know him. And I don't know what he wants from me either.

11 June

Liesl's fallen in love with an Englishman, he's immensely lean and tall and he's called Bob. She says he's very rich and went to Oxford. She talks of nothing else but him. Yesterday she said her only wish was to get away from here and go to England. I think she hopes he'll marry her. But marriage between the English and Austrian women is forbidden by the military government. She said the wretched conditions here are never going to end and she's been through too much, she can't take any more and she wants to have a life at last. I can well understand her but then I get annoyed with her because she thinks I ought to marry an Englishman too and get away from here. Of course I want to get away but so that I can go to university and I've no desire to get married at all, not even to an Englishman for a few tins of food and silk stockings. Most of the English who are here are very nice and, I believe, decent. But I'm much too young, Arthur and Bill are very nice and we often talk a lot together and laugh a lot. We often play games like 'Drop the Handkerchief' and 'Statues' in the garden. Arthur's always giving little Heinerle chocolate and a few days ago he suddenly went to

Mummy, who's still bedridden, and put some tea and biscuits on the quilt for her. She calls him 'Carrot-top' because he has such red hair and she likes him best. I think he's in love with Liesl as well, Bill too, but even more, and Arthur's terribly jealous of Bob. Bob is quite unapproachable, we once spoke a couple of words but never again, not even when I thanked him for letting Liesl have the car to bring her mother back from hospital.

14 June

My mind's still in a whirl. Jack Hamesh was here, this time he came in a jeep. Naturally, everyone in the village stared and Frau S. came over the stream twice to have a look in the garden. I took him into the garden because Mummy's in bed upstairs. We sat on the bench and at first I was all of a tremble so that he must have thought I'm mad or have a bad conscience or God knows what. And I've no idea why. I can't remember what we talked about at first but all at once we were on to books, to Thomas Mann and Stefan Zweig and Schnitzler and Hofmannsthal. I was so happy, he knows everything and he told me he never thought he'd find a young girl in Austria who'd read all that despite her Nazi upbringing. And suddenly everything was quite different and I told him everything about the books. He told me he was taken to England in a *kindertransport* with other Jewish children in '38, he was actually eighteen then but an uncle managed to arrange it, his parents were already dead. So now I know how he comes to speak such good German, then he went into the British army and now in the zones of occupation there are lots of former Germans and Austrians working in the FSS offices, because of the language and because they know conditions in the country better. We talked until evening and he kissed my hand before he left. No one's ever kissed my hand before. I'm out of my mind I'm so happy and after he'd gone I climbed up the apple tree, it was already dark and I cried my eyes out and thought I never wanted to wash my hand again.

Jack comes every day and I've never talked so much in all my life. And now he always brings books. He doesn't particularly like poetry. Mostly we talk about philosophy and history. He's very good at explaining things and I'm not shy with him at all now, I always ask him when there's something I haven't heard of. At the moment we're in the middle of Socialism and Communism (of course, if Mummy were to hear the word Communism she'd faint!), but you have to know everything exactly and study it. I'm reading *Capital* by Marx and a book by Adler.[10] I told Jack I'd like to study philosophy and he takes me seriously and thinks that's right. I've just kept quiet about my poems.

Liesl borrowed my shoes, because of Bob. I'm quite happy to lend them now and then but now she's wearing them all the time and I have to go round in my old slippers, even when Jack's here. Mummy also thinks she's being very inconsiderate. Jack thinks she's very bright and she sometimes comes over, if she has time, and then we usually have lots of laughs, he likes her a lot, they all do, of course, but it doesn't bother me. You can't have a sensible conversation with her at the moment, she's got her head in the clouds. I'm starting to have my doubts whether she'll make a good doctor, dancing and company and flirting's much more important for her. She's completely changed. I think her father's worried, too. Bob's given her a car so now she has two, an official car from the Red Cross and her own car, and Bill, who's grown quite melancholy, chauffeurs her around. He's so stupid and good-natured.

So that's the way things are. Everyone's talking about me, including all our relations, of course. 'She's going out with the Jew.' And naturally Mummy's quite worried because of all the gossip, she just can't understand what it all means to me! Because she keeps beating about the bush, I brought the topic up myself, while we were cooking today and told her that nothing was ever said between us that another person couldn't hear, she knows that herself, she feels it better than anybody. After all, she knows me! But that's not why, it's because of 'with the Jew'. And I told her I'd walk up and down through Vellach and through Hermagor ten times over with him, even if everyone gets in a stew about it, especially then.

This is the loveliest summer of my life, and even if I live to be hundred it will still be the loveliest spring and summer. Lots of people say we don't see much sign of the peace but for me it is peace, peace! People are all so terribly stupid; did they expect that, after such a disaster, a land of milk and honey would dawn from one day to the next! That the English would have nothing else in mind than to make life a bed of roses for us? God, who would have thought only a few months ago that we would even survive! Every day I go up the Goria by myself to dream, to have wonderful dreams! I'll study, work, write! I'm alive, I'm alive! Oh God, to be free and alive, even without shoes, without food, without stockings, without, no, no, it's a wonderful time!

We don't talk about Daddy any more. I don't because of Mummy and she doesn't because of us. If he really was in Prague . . . Jack says the Americans and English are releasing a lot of prisoners already but of course they don't know what the Russians are doing. Basically we know nothing. Rumours of plunder and rape come from Vienna, it's terrible. Will I be able to get to Vienna at all. When? And how? I can't stay here for ever, waiting and waiting. If the universities don't open soon, I'll have to look for work. Perhaps with the English, so we get something to eat. There's less and less. Yesterday we were allocated a ration of horse meat and two of the three tins were off. If it wasn't for Aunt Rose! At least that means we have milk for Heinerle, though he, too, is looking like a little skeleton by now, I can't understand why, for we do everything we can for him.

Notes

1   In the Gail valley in southern Carinthia, about 80 kilometres from the capital, Klagenfurt.

2   Completion of 'National Labour Service' was a prerequisite for being allowed to enter university; anyone who was 'unfit for labour service' had to do 'student substitute service', which was why she had to report to this official.

3   A school friend, not to be confused with her sister Isi (Isolde).

4   The first line of one of the poems from Rainer Maria Rilke's *Das Stundenbuch* (*The Book of Hours*).

5   The neighbour's dog.

6   A diminutive of Heinz. Her much younger brother Heinz who was only six at the time.

7   Field Security Section.

8   The final school-leaving exam which is also a qualification for university.

9 Bund deutscher Mädel (German Girls'
   League). A Nazi organization for girls;
   membership was not compulsory until 1939
   but was 'expected' of Aryan children. Up to
   14 they were in the Jungmädelbund (Young
   Girls' League); they then transferred to
   the BdM proper; they were sworn in at a
   ceremony broadcast across the nation on
   Hitler's birthday.

10 It is difficult to say whether they read
   Victor Adler, the founder of the Austrian
   Social Democratic Party, who corresponded
   with Engels, or Alfred Adler, the psychoanalyst and disciple of Freud, who was even
   more important for the Austrian labour
   movement than Freud, or—most probably—
   Max Adler (1873–1937), who in his theoretical writings and organizational work tried
   to keep open the option of an alternative to
   Stalinism.

LETTERS FROM JACK HAMESH

1

HERMAGOR, EASTER 1946

Dear Inge,

I'm sorry you weren't in. But I haven't much time since our excursion to Luggau begins at 1 o'clock.

But don't be angry with me if I leave without saying goodbye.

Enjoy your Easter holiday as well. I hope it will be possible for us to spend a holiday together some day.

I'll be back by Tuesday evening at the latest and the first thing I'll do will be to go and see you of course.

In the meantime be happy the way one ought to be at Easter.

Please don't be angry with me if I leave a few trifles here to sweeten your holiday a little (not much). I like doing it and take it as it's intended.

Once more my very, very best wishes to your parents, your brother and sister and to you, dear Inge.

See you soon
Jakob

2

HERMAGOR

16th June 1946

Dear Inge,

Now I must finally keep my promise and write to you.

Only a few days have passed and if I had to write a report to you about what has happened in the meantime here between Obervellach and Hermagor . . . really I wouldn't know what to write about.

However I won't spend too much time with those two places then but go on to Graz a bit, for you're there and above all we should talk about you and about me.

The last few days we spent together are still vividly present in my mind. Both the afternoon when we went swimming and didn't talk much, and the lovely last evening we spent together.

Above all I'm glad that I didn't offend you too much, for nothing would hurt me more than to offend you.

Pity you're not here, dear Inge. As long as you were here, I knew what I could do today or tomorrow. I would happily wait because I told myself: This evening I'll be with Inge but now time passes so monotonously, uniformly, emptily, it often makes me shudder.

Then I often think it would be nice to get out of this uniform so that I would finally be master of my own time and only then will we see how suited I am to shaping my own destiny, as far as one can shape that at all.

But you, dear Inge, have helped me in many ways. For I had already lost my belief in many things. Through you, however, I realized that you don't have to look at everything in the same light. It was only through you that I saw that it was still worth believing in people. Not in everyone, in a few, in individuals, in you.

I know it will be difficult, it's uncertain how long we'll be together, whether and when we'll see each other again is still pretty . . . but I do know one thing and that is that these days cannot be forgotten.

I often thought that we actually don't really know each other yet.

For you only rarely told me something of your past and I wasn't all that communicative either.

But one thing about you struck me. Despite the fact that you have a nice home, parents and brother and sister, you long to be alone.

I always felt the urge to get away. In time, however, I was forced to be alone but I had to get used to it. I believe we came together in this loneliness. Perhaps also liked each other because of that. But my road will take me somewhere else once more, it really frightens me just to think about it, only when it becomes a reality will I see how difficult it will be to be completely without you.

To me my future seems like a fearful labyrinth where there's no way out. But in the difficult times that lie ahead of me, and I can see them quite clearly, I will think of you and then I am sure I will find it much easier to overcome many obstacles.

A different country and different people, I don't really know, perhaps that's where I belong, for if I could decide here or there many things would be easier.

But enough of that for now. How are you dear Inge? Has everything gone well?

Are you studying a lot? What other nice things are there in the big city?

Have pity on us, we poor provincials are wasting away intellectually out here, come soon and bring me some fresh air and some new ideas. I really am longing to see you

All the best your

Jäcki

3

Villach Release Camp

27th June 1946

My dear Inge,

The first part of my journey starts at 9 a.m. today and goes direct to Naples.

After a long time I have to get used to a soldier's life again for a few days. But it won't be long before I'm out of uniform again.

A serious and decisive period of my life is beginning for me and I have to say parting from you, dear Inge, and from all the others I have grown fond of, does not make it any easier.

But I will pull myself together, for only now do I have to show how far I am capable of standing on my own two feet in a world that is almost alien to me with no family, almost without acquaintances and without friends.

But, Inge dear, it's only through having met you that I have seen that it is worthwhile fighting, even at times when it's as difficult as can be. I hope to see you again some day, for the days I spent with you were not only of great importance for me they were a turning point in my life.

Please stay well, Inge, and think of me sometimes.

I won't forget you and all your dear ones of course.

Best wishes to your parents, Isolde, Elisabeth, the Pirkers, Herr and Frau Hruss.

Jäcki

4

NAPLES,3 JULY1946

greetings from naples letter follows

jak

5

NAPLES,6 JULY 1946

6th June 1946

Dear Inge,

The days pass and still I'm sitting in Naples.

If I knew it was only for a few weeks and then I could be back with you, these days here wouldn't be so dreadful.

But just think of all the things that lie between us! Not just the distance—different countries and a different environment and different languages. How long will it be before I will be able to set off on the way back?

I hope, dear Inge, that you felt how difficult it was for me to leave you. At least you were the more composed and seemed to be the stronger one. But I don't know whether you have ever in your life really had to say goodbye to someone you were really fond of, who meant more to you than anything else, without knowing when or where you will see them again.

I have unfortunately had to do that several times.

The days on the train from Villach to Naples were the most painful I have ever spent. I didn't talk to anyone during the whole journey, I was completely self-absorbed and it cost me an extreme effort to hold back the tears that kept welling up. It was no use comforting myself and telling myself to be strong!

The days I spent with you, dear, dear Inge, were days such as I have seldom had in my life. I was glad just to see you, if I could talk to you and be together with you, dear Inge, then I felt what you and your dear home and your lovely garden meant to me.

I truly feel a longing for Obervellach and Hermagor, for that is where I have left you and the Pirkers, whom I truly love, where I left other friends who are dear to me.

Now I am so far away from you and tomorrow I will be even farther away.

In one or two days we will board ship, then it'll be off to that troubled country where it seems peace can never come. Here I've met other fellow soldiers who are setting off on the same journey. Many of them are much more confident than I am, they see Palestine as the only country where the problem that has been waiting a thousand years for a solution can be solved.

Perhaps they're right. Until now, I've never joined in those discussions for they arouse violent and bitter arguments.

It's a long time, almost four years, since I saw Palestine and I would find it difficult to express an opinion. So I remain silent and just listen to the flood of words pouring over me.

National honour, a Jewish state. Palestine the only answer, salvation for hundreds of thousands of refugees, economic development and cultural progress, the mission of the Jewish people, an example, etc. Those are the slogans buzzing round but which barely penetrate my consciousness in my present state. For good or ill I live in another world and, if I may say so, have risen above all that.

Others say I'm running away, avoiding a decision.

But I can't change anything. I live with you and only with you, and that's the way things are.

I hope you understand me, you always understood me and I was proud to have such a dear, sweet friend as you.

Dear Inge even now that I'm far away from you, I'm still with you.

For you must have felt what you are to me and how much I love and need you. You helped me and are still helping me today, for the idea of seeing you again makes these moments easier to bear, so stay in good health and give my best wishes to your parents, your sister and all the others who loved me and whom I loved.

With all my best wishes, your Jäcki.

6

TEL AVIV

24. 7. 1946

Dear, dear Inge,

I've finally found time to write a few lines to you. I haven't had a single quiet minute since I had to leave you. You can't imagine how much I suffered during my journey from beautiful Carinthia to Palestine.

Now almost a month has passed and I still haven't managed to pull myself together. I've had to fight my way through some pretty difficult times during my life but it seems to me that nothing in my previous experiences can compare with the last few days and weeks.

Completely uprooted, with nothing to hold on to, something I've never been through before, these last few weeks have been the most terrible time I've had to go through. Do forgive me, dear, kind Inge, for writing things like this, I'd love to have something happy to tell you but every line I add brings new pain and new suffering. I can't describe my true situation to you, I feel as if I've sunk incredibly low, a disaster which I perhaps alone sense, for I alone experience it, experience it all on my own, as alone as I've never been before, I wasn't even as devastated by the death of my mother as I have been by this last month. There's not much I can write and tell you, for I'm still in a state in which it's impossible to start on any scheme and starting something is not easy here. No apartments, no jobs and no prospect of improvement. One thing is clear to me even now: I'm going to have to work very hard, at first I'm going to have to accept any work just to keep body and soul together. Life in the army has done nothing to prepare me for this struggle. Here, all my plans have come to nothing, I'm faced with completely new conditions, facts I could never have foreseen. Day after day I become more and more aware how decisive my last step was.

Please forgive me for saying nothing about the journey, nothing about my life but I find it impossible. I am in such an overwrought state that for the moment I can't bring myself to do anything. But I am constantly thinking of you all the time, Inge dear. Not a day passes when I don't look at your picture which is still in [unreadable] which I leaf through now and then. For I still can't read and who knows when I'll be able to look at and assess things more calmly again.

Where are the days together with you in your dear, nice little room, in your lovely garden? I remember those wonderful hours again and again and even now I can hardly write since the mere thought of you and your dear home brings tears to my eyes.

To live alone is terrible, especially when you have to part from people you've become fond of and you must have felt that I have become fond of you, respect you and think highly of you.

There is just one thing that still hurts. You didn't say a single word about seeing each other again or about staying or about meeting again somewhere, some day.

I know it will be difficult but the hope that it can happen in the future should have made us talk about it. Even at the last minute in the main street as I walked towards you, crying as our car drove past you, even then you said nothing about it and I really wanted to hear it from you lips, dear Inge. We will meet again.

Give your dear little sister my best wishes, I saw her on the last day when I said goodbye to the dear Pirker family, I couldn't look her in the eye, for otherwise . . .

Give my best wishes to your mother and your father as well, tell them that I always felt at ease and happy among them and in their home, tell them that whatever may have happened, whatever I have suffered in Austria, I, with thousands of others, will never let myself forget the friendship and kindness I felt in your home.

Dear, dear Inge give my best wishes to dear Elisabeth as well and to other people who were nice and kind to me.

But above all, dear little Inge, I send you my love and assure you that in you I have found a person whom I will never forget, unless you don't want to hear from me any more. My situation is bad, tomorrow it will be even worse, please think of your Jäcky so that I can at least have that comfort.

Jäcki

Reply soon.

Best wishes to the Pirkers.

Letter on its way. Best wishes to the Erbers.

7

TEL AVIV, 24 JULY 1946 [?]

> To my dear Inge
>> a memento
> A great woman
> A brilliant researcher
> and an ideal mother
> Recall sometimes the happy hours
> we spent together
>
>> Jäcki

8

Tel Aviv, 1st 11. 46

(I)

Dear, dear Inge,

At last I can reply. Forgive me for making you wait so long but with the best will in the world I couldn't reply to your first letter. I'm not angry with you, for why, when you have to struggle with so many difficulties yourself, should I take offence at your comforting me, who am now thousands of kilometres away from you.

But your second letter shows me that there is still a close human relationship between us, that you haven't entirely forgotten me. I'm really glad you've written me such a nice letter. It spoke to me of the Inge I have never forgotten, from what you write I can see that you are still the same dear Inge whom I love above all else and whom I have always respected and thought highly of.

Take these lines as they are intended. You know what I felt for you and how much I would love to be with you. Only today, now that I have not been with you for almost half a year, can I really feel what our farewell meant.

I was really delighted to receive your letter, at the same time, however, I was overcome with sadness, for knowing how much you've had to suffer, fighting all on your own in the hurly-burly of our cruel times, all that made me even sadder. How happy I was when I could be together with you, at the time when you were still living with your dear parents, in your lovely room, at the time when you still knew nothing of all the terrible reality. And how much happier I would be to be with you today, to hear your dear voice again, to share your worries and at the same time to defy these times with a laugh. For we understood each other at a time when none of the rest could free themselves from people's hatred for each other. How glad I am that you managed to overcome your fears, how difficult those few weeks must have been but the fact that despite everything you have a positive attitude to life, whatever form it may take today, have not bowed to necessity, however tempting it might seem, is a sign of your strength, of your will to live and, not least, of your confidence things must change, for that is why you have resolved to live, that it why you were able to win the struggle with yourself.

There is really no great difference between these critical weeks and months, which you had to struggle through just as I did, and, if I am not mistaken, thousands and thousands of other people of our age. But you and I in particular. While I was still in Carinthia I wrote you a letter, which you probably didn't receive until after I'd left, saying how much our situations are similar. We are both alone, the reasons may be different but the consequences are the same.

P.S. Please don't be angry because I'm typing this letter.

I know what you think about that but my handwriting is not always legible and I want you to understand.

Don't read these lines as an article just because they're printed . . .

(II)

I am glad that even in my absence I can do something to give you pleasure and I hope that you will enjoy this modest little casket.

Now, dear Inge, you ask how I am . . .

After reading your letter, hearing about your difficulties, I'm ashamed to complain at all. My first letter must have sounded quite desperate and, without wanting to pretend that everything is turning out fine, we here don't have the kind of worries that are weighing you down. What oppresses me is simply the feeling of being abandoned, the loneliness, the yearning for all the dear friends I had to leave so suddenly.

Of course, I too, have to struggle with difficulties but at the moment I can say that the most difficult days are behind me. I'm working. That alone is a lot today. Even if not everything is as I would wish, although I had different plans, I am still glad to have an honest occupation, to be earning my living and not be dependent on the help and charity of others. The transition from soldier to civilian wasn't easy. Gone is the protective uniform, the privileges, the false self-confidence which is mostly based on the sense of belonging to the military, now you're on your own, no longer dependent and pushed around.

I would have liked to have gone to university but unfortunately that's completely out of the question here, however, I study in the evenings, read a lot, there are books and evening classes, and education and knowledge are not always dependent on letters after your name, although to be honest that's what my mother and I always dreamt of. However, since I live in a world in which not all wishes can be granted, I have to subordinate myself to the prevailing conditions, and since nothing in the world is free, earn my daily bread by the sweat of my brow.

In your last letter you ask me to trust you and to tell you more about my life here. So far I haven't kept anything secret, Inge dear, my trust in you is as great as it always was. But in our life so much is dependent on externals and I was afraid . . . You knew me as a soldier, we spent happy times together, we talked about various problems of our times and about our personal opinions. However, somehow I could always feel my uniform, the position I had at the time, my work at that time; I lived in a different world, but now, when I have really gone back to life, to everyday reality, only now can I ask myself: How did people see you then, what was their opinion of you?

What was the decisive factor in my relationship with others . . . Doubts arise, did they see the person in me or the uniform? Did they respect me or the power behind me . . . Don't get me wrong, that's the only way I can see things. See them in their context. As long as no one can give me an answer to that, as long as I don't know the answer myself, I will be in doubt. Help me to find the answer. Write and tell me what you think of all that.

P.S. My typewriter doesn't work properly, I'm typing without a ribbon just with a carbon copy, that's why it looks the way it does.

(III)

Do I have any prospect of returning to Austria? I think so, though at the moment everything is still uncertain, no normal conditions, no Austr. Consulate, although that is not of itself important. Nor is the situation in Austria decisive. Political developments, the people's attitude, etc.

There is a lot about that you can write and tell me. You're living in Vienna and it is that city above all that will determine the future of Austria, if not the future of Central Europe. At the moment there is what one might almost call a 'cult' of Vienna. But there is one thing we mustn't forget. What happened there simply must not be allowed to happen again. A new Vienna must arise, a free, progressive Vienna, and that means above all a new attitude . . . not just new houses. For mental and moral rubble is much more difficult to clear away, a compulsory work programme will not solve it alone, although it can make an important contribution, but an immense process of education, political enlightenment, the exposure of the real reasons and not an escape into mysticism.

I lived for twenty years in Vienna, loved it and felt it, only in 1938 were my eyes opened, I realized I'd been living in a dream world. In your first letter you wrote that all your hope is fixed on Vienna . . . With no illusions but with great belief . . . much will depend on you, cities are very attractive but can also be very dangerous.

I hope you will succeed in everything you wish for and plan to do. Your studies will determine your further future, it all only makes sense when you manage to make practical use of your knowledge and skills in life. Then you will know why you went to university, why you put up with all the adversities. I can understand your doubts only too well, there are many who will go under in this ideological struggle, you will be tormented by many a disappointment but it is your future. Our world!

We frequently spoke about that, to you I must have seemed like a heretic mocking everything people hold most sacred . . . but not everything was meant to be taken like that, I also had high regard for the values of our time, admired the achievements of our civilization but where did all that lead us? Today we are standing on ruins, without a home, without parents, without a homeland, without hope and, worst of all, without a future.

You are absolutely right when you maintain that at bottom we all long for the comfortable bourgeois existence of the 'much-hated' middle classes. Me too: Me especially! For I lacked what other people possessed their whole life through without appreciating it.

I felt it in your home and in Dr Pirker's; but that's all long gone . . . and unfortunately in your last letter you added that sentence that you feel as if all the bridges behind you have collapsed. Have I been living in illusions again? Was our life together just a chance episode?

I felt it was something much deeper, perhaps I take things too seriously. But for me it wasn't just an encounter, for me it was proof that despite everything that has overtaken our two peoples there is still a way—the way of love and understanding.

Thank you very much for passing on my regards to all my friends. I often see your parents in my mind's eye and in thought I go again through every single second I spent in your home. They were beautiful moments amid the general misery. A relationship developed such as I would never have dreamt of, one can be pleasantly surprised in life. Now that you are a long way away from your parents I will write to them myself. I want them to know that they have a grateful friend who appreciates having been shown love and friendship.

What stage has your father's affair reached?

Is he already working as a teacher again? I would very much like to be a teacher, a profession that would satisfy me, that would set me a task that might be crowned with success. But that is just another wish. What is dear Isi doing? Is she still at school in Villach? And little Heinz?

Now I'll have to stop, Inge dear.

I've tried to answer the most important questions.

And next time will you write a very full letter, about your studies about your free time, your friends, I'm interested in everything, everything.

The most personal bit in pen and ink.

Stay healthy and strong, dear little Inge. I'm thinking of you all the time and am always ready to help you in any way I can. For if I can talk to you, I'm glad, if I manage to comfort you, to help you, I feel happy.

Let new bridges be built, for my road leads to you, Inge dear, and don't write to me again that being free makes one happy.

Were you so tied down when we were together?

Remain my dear friend whom I need so badly and love very, very much and cannot forget. Think of me sometimes and write soon.

Love and best wishes from your

Jäcki

9

Tel Aviv, 13th Nov. 1946

Dear, dear Inge,

Your letter of 24th inst. arrived today. I can't tell you how delighted I am. You know yourself, Inge dear, how valuable to me the least news from you is.

Not many days now and the second postwar Christmas will be upon us. I sent off a letter to your parents only a few days ago and in it I wrote to you at the same time.

But I'll send you a few lines as well, for whenever I can say a few words to you yourself I feel so close to you and your surroundings, which I love so much and which it was so hard to leave. And how much more now when the loveliest festival of the year is approaching. Things look pretty dismal and unfortunately there is not much prospect of them changing soon.

But I will join you in your confidence and hope with you. Things have to change, Inge dear, otherwise all the terrible suffering we've been through will have been in vain. We will have to find the forces that can take the world out of this chaos and to a better future. Once more I found a ray of hope in your letter, for the fact that you believe in progress and an improvement, despite everything you have had to suffer in recent times, is proof that it is worth living and fighting and hoping.

Unfortunately Austria is recovering very slowly. I don't know exactly where the blame lies since the reports and newspapers don't give me much insight into conditions but it seems to me that their plight has completely broken the people, unresisting, hopelessness and a lack of faith have driven people into an 'I-couldn't-care-less' mood. And for a nation that is a truly tragic situation.

Dear Inge, I think of you every day, again and again I recall some trifle that gave you and me pleasure. How I would love to be together with you, how lovely it would be to talk to you, go for walks, visit the friends we were both fond of. Now that Christmas is so close, how I would love to be in your lovely room together with your dear parents or your dear sister and little Heinzi.

It was kind of you to write to me about him and tell me that he sometimes asks after me and can't understand why I haven't been to see you for so long.

I hope this letter finds you well in your lovely new home, which is to be a surprise for you now. How I would love to have been there, to see you happy, to see you moving in the lovely dress you were wearing when we gave our party together. But I'm glad anyway to know you are at home, where everyone loves you, everyone is proud of you, everyone is asking you questions and, half irritated, you fend them off with a laugh and basically you're happy to tease all your loved ones a bit.

How I would love to see you again, putting your dear little hand in mine, to talk with you about the hard times, perhaps the hardest people have ever had to go through.

Time is pressing Inge dear. Christmas is near and I want this letter to arrive on time.

I've written this letter in a hurry, please don't be angry that I can't answer all your questions but there's sure to be more in my next letter. Enjoy yourself with your dear parents, who love you above all else, enjoy yourself with dear Isi, who is such a kind-hearted soul, enjoy yourself with your dear little brother. Be glad that you can celebrate Christmas with all those who are dearest to you.

But think of me a little as well! When you're all gathered round the table, let me be there with you, even if far from you, and accept my very best wishes, my gratitude and my love,

From: your Jäcki—always thinking of you

10

TEL AVIV, 23 JUNE 1947

Love and best wishes your

Jaky

11

Tel Aviv, 16th July 1947

Dear Inge,

Our weary correspondence has finally got going again. Of course, I realize that the times and conditions can often have the effect of interrupting it but that doesn't matter. In fact, it makes me even more pleased when you don't forget that you have a far-off friend, who is always delighted to hear from you, who is always thinking of you and who always wishes he could see you again.

It was a really nice letter but not only that, it was honest, detailed, open, friendly and intelligent. Whenever I read your letters I can't help admiring you again. Not many girls of your age would be capable of analyzing their own times and their own problems the way you do. In these years of trial you have learnt things, have made progress intellectually and in human terms, while the majority of your contemporaries have stood still and, what is worse, they will be incapable of further development.

Your last letter arrived a few days before your birthday. Believe me, on 25 June I was there with you, in your lovely home, was sitting there again with you, your dear mother and your father, with Isi and Heinzi. In joyful mood, happily immersed in an interesting conversation with you. I simply imagined it, took myself back to 1946, forgetting completely that in the meantime twelve long months have passed. And I really managed it.

I sent my telegram a couple of days before your birthday. I hope it arrived in time. I sent it to your home, assuming you would at least be celebrating your coming of age with your family.

But your urge for independence asserted itself again and you stayed in Vienna to reach your majority alone and solitary.

In this letter I'll try to talk less about general political or social problems and more about myself about my environment, my leisure activities, Palestine, about people here and various other things that will interest you.

If you ask me whether I'm content, or even happy, I would answer the first with a 'yes', the second, however, with a resounding 'no'.

I'm content because someone who at the present time has work with which he can earn a living, who doesn't need to get on other people's nerves, that is to say, is not a burden on those around him, can and must be content. I've had various jobs here already. In a leather factory and in an office, out in the fields and as a waiter.

At the moment, I'm trying to get the brick machine going that I told you about in Austria. There are great difficulties, of course. Here, you have to be able to do everything to get on.

The attitude to work here is quite different from in Europe. My mother dreamt of other things, of course.

But who expected there would ever be such a collapse of all traditional middle-class ideas? Such a transformation of conditions?

Who could foresee this immense intellectual and cultural decline?

Who would have believed that in 1938 they would see a child wandering round the world alone just because it had been born a Jew?

Who would have thought that those responsible for a child's upbringing and development, that is its father and mother, would die miserably in some gas chamber?

It was a cruel time—a time we can hardly understand today. The destruction was so massive, an incredible amount rained down on us in those years.

So that's why I'm content. I could just as well be rotting in some mass grave in Poland or Germany or even in my OLD MOTHER COUNTRY of Austria.

But I'm not happy. I have lost much of the joy of life people of my age are supposed to have. I'm alone a lot. I have found some friends, mostly from Vienna but they've all been through similar or even worse experiences. None of them can enjoy life any more, we try to forget, immerse ourselves in silence and thus bury ourselves all the more in the past we can't forget.

Who can forget their parents? Their brothers and sisters, their friends? Who can forget the land they come from?

Can you understand all that, Inge dear? Does it make you impatient when I write about it?

I can change the subject but then I wouldn't write anything more about myself. I'd have to be dishonest, give free rein to my thought machine and simply switch off emotion.

But then I wouldn't be myself . . . A person has to live, however. Any other view is wrong and drives one to the most absurd things. We've both been through it. War, hatred, racial theory and other achievements of the twentieth century, last but not least the ATOM BOMB, which is not particularly life-affirming for young people today.

That is why I have a positive attitude towards the struggle to survive, that is, not simply to dream of all the things I could have been, how many opportunities I lost, all the things I might have achieved . . . if the years 1938–45 had not been. But they were and they have put their stamp on us and on me.

Therefore I work, I'm glad that I can clothe and feed myself properly. I forgo nothing. I read, study, go to concerts, go to the cinema, laugh and dance quite often. As far as possible I take advantage of all the opportunities our culture and civilization provide. Go with the times, so to speak, but also against them when necessary, that is also important, especially today.

Fitting in again wasn't easy. So far I've managed it. The soldier inside me has died. Perhaps I never was a proper one, you probably noticed that.

I always tried not to let my humanity wither away. Otherwise I would probably have behaved differently in the position and function I had in Hermagor and in Austria.

Palestine as it is today is a new, and awakening country.

Just like any country that starts to feel its strength, Palestine will have to overcome enormous difficulties.

Intentionally or unintentionally, this little country has taken centre stage in world politics. Many refuse to admit that.

There's oil here, the Suez Canal, the way to India. Jerusalem, Christ was born here, the Jews used to live here, for centuries now the Arabs have been vegetating here, living a wretched life you would hardly believe possible.

The Ten Commandments were revealed here, everyone who believes in God, whether Christ, Jehovah or Allah, comes on pilgrimage here.

As you can see, the tangled situation here is not uncomplicated. I'm not a religious person, you know that as well as I do, I'm just trying to explain the historical background to the problem of the Jews.

Ever since they were driven out of Palestine and had to live in the Diaspora, the Jews had one hope: to return to the land promised them by God.

Of all the peoples of the ancient world, only the Jews are left. And here I do have to bring in religion. The Jews were the first to believe in one God. The Ten Commandments were the basis of the law, the Torah or the Book of Teaching their spiritual nourishment.

Zionism, which is demanding the return of the Jews to Palestine today, is not based on that traditional longing of the Jews alone. Above all, there are reasons that go much deeper.

The impossibility of assimilation, the eternal anti-Semitism, that evil of all evils, the rootlessness and homelessness of the Jews, the unhealthy social and economic structure of the Jews within the various peoples, finally Hitler and Nazi Germany, have shown Zionism the arguments and the only possible way.

(I won't write any more about that. If you have any questions, I'm happy to answer them at length.)

The population consists of 1,200,000 Arabs (that isn't a precise figure since it's difficult to carry out a census of the Arabs as a large part of them live as nomads), 700,000 Jews and 70,000 Christians. The languages are Arabic and Hebrew which, unlike old Latin and Greek, has become a living language again.

English is taught as a second language in schools.

Tel Aviv is the largest city here. 250,000 inhabitants. Thirty years ago, there was a hill of sand here, standing on it today is Tel Aviv which means Hill of Spring.

Agriculture is modern, mechanized, villages are much closer in style to towns than in Europe. The rural population is not backward, it consists mostly of former students, middle-class people and intellectuals.

Agriculture is mostly organized in collective units.

We have a subtropical climate here. That is, there are hotter spots on this earth but from June to October it is often oppressively hot here too. But the climate does not hinder the development of the country. New villages spring up out of the sand. Water is sought and keeps being found, new springs to push back the desert.

Trees are being planted on ground that has been neglected for millennia. Schools, libraries, evening classes, workers' study groups, unions, conservatories, a university, colleges of advanced technology, everything that is part of a modern world is slowly but surely being developed here.

The living standard of the Arabs has risen a hundredfold and it is a lie when people say the Jews have made them landless. Not one Arab has had to leave his land.

On the contrary, since the immigration of the Jews, the Arabs have increased in numbers, hospitals, hygienic facilities, antenatal and postnatal care, all that is the pioneering work of the once homeless, expelled, hated Jews.

We don't have the kind of winters we remember from Europe here.

But we do have clouds, rain, thunder and lightning here from October to the beginning of June. Very, very rarely snow, in Jerusalem it was a sensation when children were throwing snowballs a few years ago.

Tel Aviv is modern in the truest sense of the word. Architecture, clothes, pace of life, etc.

Here you can find everything, good or bad, you find in any big city.

Jerusalem is more conservative, quieter. On Saturday, you really could imagine you were in a holy town. Not even a car is to be seen.

Haifa is a port. A very beautiful situation, more beautiful than Tel Aviv since it lies on the slopes of a mountain.

Jews and Arabs live in Jerusalem, also in Haifa, in Tel Aviv only Jews. The girls here are very taste-fully dressed. Not flamboyantly. During the day most of the men wear shorts, in the evening well-tailored long trousers and white or self-coloured shirts. Without ties. You can't tell their social back-ground from their clothes. The cafes are very lively. In the evening the people stream to the beach in their thousands to enjoy a cool drink with Vien-nese music.

Lots of people listen to music here. The con-cert halls are always full.

The favourite composers here are: Mozart, Schubert, Beethoven, then Chopin, Tchaikovsky, Dvorak, Smetana, also Ravel and a few new local names in music enjoy great popularity.

As you can see, Inge dear, Palestine lives despite everything. Here the Jews have their last chance, at least as long as the other nations cannot renounce their hatred of the Jews this is the only place where the surviving Jews from Europe can find refuge and a new life.

There's lots more I could write. But this letter's too long already. There are still some things in your letter I have to answer but it's too late for that today. I'll wait for your reply and then I'll reply in full.

Please write soon and at length. Everything, everything interests me. About you and your parents, about Isi and Heinzi.

About Austria, Vienna and about the beautiful Gail valley, where you are probably staying at the moment.

With best wishes
in friendship from your
<u>Jäcki</u>

Dear Inge,

Don't be angry with me because I've preferred typing to writing by hand again. I think I'm making it much easier for you to read. Don't look on it as disrespect or disparagement. I had so much to write and typed, it's much clearer.

So don't be angry, my dear Inge.

In the early summer of 1945, the eighteen-year-old
Ingeborg Bachmann met a soldier of the British 8th
Army. The first time she saw him, in the offices of
the Field Security Section (FSS) in Hermagor,
Carinthia,[1] she thought him 'short and on the ugly
side'; but later, after they had talked for some time,
'suddenly everything was quite different'. No other
person would bring about such a change in her way
of thinking, indeed in her whole existence, for
their encounter coincided with a singular moment
in history. The evocative language in the second
part of her diary—the weeks immediately after the
end of the war—gives the meeting with Jack
Hamesh, as the soldier was called, a significance
that was to remain with her for the rest of her life:

'This is the loveliest summer of my life, and even if
I live to be hundred—it will still be the loveliest
spring and summer' (p. 16). Twenty years later, in
her novel *Das Buch Franza* (The Book of Franza), she
would recall the time in 1945 when they were freed
from the war as 'the loveliest spring'.

For Hamesh, too, the encounter was no less
significant: Bachmann made him aware of the
sense of his survival and helped him to escape from
the 'loneliness' which other exiles speak of as the
fundamental experience of their persecution.[2] He
believed he could see in her a similar loneliness,
even if one caused by different conditions (Letter
of 16 June 1946, pp. 24–8).

'The Loveliest Summer' and What Preceded It

The different conditions leading to Bachmann's
loneliness (even though she had a 'nice home'[3]) are
documented in her diary. The first part, the actual
'war' diary, describes how, along with other young
women, she withdrew from militarized Nazi society and its dictatorship of terror in education and
headed instead for freedom. Her courage and her
refusal to compromise are allied to her books: in

the garden of the Klagenfurt house she read, with death all around her, Rilke's *Stundenbuch* (Book of Hours) and Baudelaire's *Fleurs du Mal* (Flowers of Evil). And she was prepared to desert when she found herself exposed to the murderous consequences of Nazi education in the teacher-training college: 'These grown-ups, these high-and-mighty "educators", who want to let us get killed' (p. 8).

The second part of Bachmann's diary—written around the end of May and in June 1945—is about the immediate post-war period in Obervellach.[4] She fled to the village above Hermagor, to the small house her father had inherited, with her mother (Olga Bachmann, née Haas, 1901–98), her sister Isolde (b. 1928) and her brother Heinz (b. 1939). Her father (Matthias Bachmann, 1895–1973), a teacher by profession, had been an officer in the army since the beginning of the war; he rejoined the family in August 1945 after a brief period as a prisoner of war with the Americans.

Bachmann's early short story 'Das Honditsch-kreuz. Eine Erzählung aus dem Jahre 1813' (The Honditsch Cross: A Story from 1813; 1943) is set in that area of southern Carinthia; the cross of the title is not far from her home. As a seventeen-year-old, she situated her story—about the world of war and the Nazi ideology of a border war—in the region of her homeland closest to her: Obervellach in the Gail valley is the land of her childhood. In *Das Buch Franza*, her childhood myth is called 'Galicia' and the chapter in which Franza remembers the time of liberation from war and Nazi rule in the spring and summer of 1945 is called 'Return to Galicia'.

'Das Honditschkreuz' is set during the war of liberation against Napoleon and it mainly takes place in the mixed-language area[5] of Obervellach and Hermagor. The young writer is less concerned with the liberation from Napoleonic rule than with the mania of nationalism which makes people take leave of their senses and turns them into madmen and murderers. Here, for the first time in Bachmann's writing, we find the longing to cross fixed frontiers, the image of the bridge as an ideal and the portrayal of war as a place of murder. She completed the story in 1943, the same year in which the Nazi 'Borderland Exhibition'—which marshalled all aspects of the military ideology of a frontier struggle—took place in Klagenfurt.

Part of Bachmann's distancing from the 'German racial community', which preceded her meet-

ing with Hamesh, was to read books banned
and burnt by the Nazis. They became a shibboleth
by which the soldier of the British Army who had
returned to Austria, and the eighteen-year-old
student who had just completed secondary school,
recognized each other. It was the books from the
world of yesterday which suddenly changed the
conversation between them: in her diary entry for
14 June 1945 (pp. 13–18), she wrote, 'suddenly everything was quite different'. The same entry reveals
how a future opened up for her: how she became
aware that what was happening must never be lost;
that it must become a measure of her future life. She
publicly acknowledged her friendship with Hamesh
and declared that she'd 'walk up and down through
Vellach and through Hermagor ten times over with
him, even if everyone gets in a stew about it,' yes,
'especially then' because both in the village and in
the town people still took offence at 'the Jew'.

In their first conversation about books she has
read she mentions Mann, Zweig, Schnitzler and
Hofmannsthal, and Hamesh is surprised to find
someone who has read 'all that despite her Nazi
upbringing'.[6] Her diary shows how attentively she
listened to him and to his completely different life

story. In her description, the end of the 14 June meeting is like a dream picture of a new coming together after the catastrophe, like a picture Chagall never painted: after a Jew, driven out of Austria in 1938, has kissed her hand, the eighteen-year-old daughter of a Carinthian Nazi family climbs up into an apple tree that night and cries, thinking she never wants to wash her hand again.[7]

It was as if the books began to live, for those that Bachmann had read and those Hamesh gave her to read ('Marx and Adler', writing branded by the Nazis as 'Jewish-Bolshevist') and, above all, the way they read *together*, all show the new openness of the world after the military liberation from Nazi rule. Hamesh, born in Vienna in 1920—where, it is possible, he was called Jakob Fünfer since 'hamesh' means 'five' in Hebrew—told her the story of his flight from Austria, which she recorded in her diary. In 1938, he managed to flee to England in a *kinder-transport* with other Jewish children even though he was already eighteen. She asks him when there's something she hasn't heard of and she realizes that, with 'the Jew' and these books, she is moving away from the world she grew up in and that her mother would faint if she heard them talking.

It was in people like her, willing to distance themselves from what they had heard and to listen to other stories, that the survivors of the Shoah put their hope after 1945. Several years after he met Bachmann in 1948 post-war Vienna, Paul Celan recalled the poem 'In Ägypten' (In Egypt) that he had dedicated to her: for him, she was the 'foundation of life', 'also because you are and remain the justification for my speaking'.[8]

The Break with the Wartime World of her Father's Generation

The first part of the diary, from the last months of the war in Klagenfurt, contains the description of Bachmann's desertion from a country kept under occupation by the 'high-and-mighty "educators"'. The final sentence is: 'No, there's no point in talking to grown-ups any more' (p. 9).

The 'hated teacher-training college', for which she had to register in order to avoid being assigned to compulsory labour in Poland—presumably it was the National Labour Service—was an organizing centre of the Nazi ideology of homeland and

ethnic nationality. The name 'Anderluh' mentioned
several times in the diary represents the way in
which Nazi education and ethnic German culture
had gone completely over the top during Hitler's
'total war'. The person Bachmann probably had in
mind is Anton Anderluh (1896–1975), principal of
the teacher-training college in Klagenfurt from
1938 to 1945. He was well known as an expert on
folk song, conductor of many male and female
voice choirs, head of the *Gau*[9] committee for folk
music in Carinthia, regional head of the Reich
Chamber of Music for Carinthia and, as established
by a commission set up by the Klagenfurt senate in
June 2008, 'more' than just a 'follower of the Nazi
regime of terror'.[10]

After the First World War, the border conflicts
and the politically exploited 'defensive struggle'
against Yugoslavia's territorial claims meant that
enthusiasm for 'home defence' was particularly
strong in Carinthia. This made it easy for Nazi
officials to steer the patriotic sentiments towards
support for the war effort. The murderous consequences of this ethnic cult of the homeland is
the subject of the so-called dream chapter in

Bachmann's *Malina*. In it, the 'origin' of the destruction is seen in the 'topography' of a Carinthian landscape.[11] The theme of this first nightmarish scene—unmistakably the Wörthersee near Klagenfurt—is the hushing up of the crimes committed at that spot. The dreaming woman has a suspicion of 'which lake it might be': the soulful male voice choirs, once standing on the ice in the middle of the lake, are now gone. And the lake, which cannot be seen, is fringed with the many graveyards. Her father is standing beside her; he takes his hand off her shoulder when the gravedigger comes up to them. He tries to forbid the man from speaking; and, after moving his lips soundlessly for a while, he speaks only one sentence: 'That is the graveyard of the murdered daughters./He shouldn't have told me that and I cried bitter tears.'[12]

The war diary, in which Bachmann describes the destructive nature of her father's generation, is fundamental to understanding the passages on the father-daughter drama developed in the subsequent dream scenes of *Malina*, and which explode into a panorama of violence that in some mysterious way brings them together in an ominous silence. 'My father, I say to him, I wouldn't have betrayed you, I wouldn't have told anyone,' Bachmann writes in the dream of the great gas chamber of the world, the one immediately after the Carinthia dream.[13]

The father-son theme of late nineteenth/early twentieth century literature is, in Bachmann's writing, overwritten by the murder of the daughter. After 1945, we can no longer ignore the fact that the war of the fathers and sons was not fought outside the family but, rather, destroyed the foundations of civilian and family life. In the war diary, the focus is still on the murderous Nazi educators outside the family; but the later the book, the more urgent is Bachmann's debate with the 'father', whom she presents as a social institution, a 'great figure', a 'figure that carries out what society carries out.'[14] However, as she writes 'my father' (or 'our family' elsewhere), we are compelled to see ourselves included in this literary discussion on the connection between fathers and violence and on families who remain silent.

A text that has only survived in fragments and that confronts us, in the fictional first-person narrator, with the dilemma of talking about 'our family', was probably written while Bachmann worked on *Todesarten* (Manners of Death) in the second half of the 1960s. The narrative fragment *Der Tod wird kommen* (Death will come) is about the impossibility of betraying one's own family 'with its festering boils', even though we are 'allowed to see more of our family' than 'of any other': 'I have acquired a big eye for our family, a big ear for its languages, acquired a big silence about so much that is to be hushed up from the immediate proximity.'[15]

'*I simply can't understand why you blush and tremble when you're telling the truth.*'

In her diary, Bachmann records in detail how she was interrogated about her membership in the 'Bund deutscher Mädel', an organization that was part of the Hitler Youth. In this entry, she is most concerned about the fact that 'I blushed bright red and I was so desperate I went even redder,' even though she could quite truthfully respond with a 'No' to Hamesh's question about whether she had been a leader in the BdM; she had not been to meetings and gatherings (pp. 10–11) since she turned fourteen. She simply couldn't understand 'why you blush and tremble when you're telling the truth'—as if the psychosomatic reaction indicates uncertainty and shame which lies outside the Yes or No of her answers. However inappropriate this body language might seem, as a writer Bachmann took it seriously. In her literary work as well as in her theoretical essays, she constantly examined the connection between 'politics' and 'physiology',[16] as if there was something, in the 'completely incomprehensible realm', that suggested a deeper level of reality. In her first review of Heinrich Böll's *Der Zug war pünktlich* (The Train was on Time, 1949), a representative work of post-war West German literature, she insisted that we acknowledge our repressed thoughts and instincts, and indirectly derived from this what she felt should be an ethics of post-war literature. About Böll's story she wrote that the author only rises 'above the average mindless war story' where 'things the author has not invoked, not called on, "fall upon" his book "without warning"'.[17]

As Bachmann saw it, the authorial 'I' has to expose itself to that which has been hushed up or silenced and then present it within the text. The literary structures that correspond to this idea can be found in the dream sequences of *Ein Geschäft mit Träumen* (A Deal in Dreams, 1952), her first radio play, and in the dream chapter in *Malina* as well as in her theoretical reflections on the 'story *in* the "I" '[18] or in the idea of a combination of music and literature 'that pursues the unseemly right into its sleep'.[19] The first poem in her first collection, writen on the theme of departure, contains the lines: 'a red trail / remains in the water, sleep lays you down there, / . . . / and your senses fade.'[20]

Is the reaction which she could not understand and which irritated her perhaps also connected with the fact that she was so alone? For what was even more incomprehensible was that, apart from her, hardly anyone else was trembling (unless it was out of fear for their own safety) and that hardly anyone else blushed for shame. During the Nazi era, almost all the teachers in Carinthia— the 'high-and-mighty "educators" '—were members of the Nazi Party, as her father had been since 1932. Which was why, after his return from the war in August 1945, he was not allowed to work as a teacher for a while.

Jack Hamesh's Letters

In the letters we see Hamesh, who did not have the opportunity to go to university, although that was what he and his mother had always 'dreamt of' (8, p. 44), as a young intellectual whom, with his knowledge and experiences, we can place alongside the well-known writers of the Shoah. And his letters also show him as a lover, one whose love Bachmann could not return. The impossibility of this union was a repetition of the trauma caused by his earlier experiences of loss. That she did not want to abandon him can be deduced indirectly from his answers to her letters, for so far it has proved impossible to trace her letters any more than Hamesh himself. Before he left Carinthia for Palestine, she went from Graz, where she was at university, back to Obervellach to say goodbye to him.[21] She could not, however, say the word that would have called him back. A historical background and the idea of an exemplary relationship are not enough for love and a life together.[22] She avoided this drama in the 'Galicia' chapter of *Das Buch Franza* and replaced Hamesh's story—perhaps because she was too closely affected by it—with a literary figure whose personality is closely related to but is also the direct opposite of Hamesh's. That Hamesh was not forgotten in Bachmann's family is evident from an unlikely memento that still survives: a piece of wrapping paper from a food parcel that Hamesh sent to Bachmann, presumably at Christmas 1946, from Israel to Vienna and then took a month-long detour by sea via Australia.[23]

Despite his occasionally uncertain spelling and grammar, Hamesh formulates the experiences of an exile with a precision and vivid imagery that recall Jean Améry's essays in *Jenseits von Schuld und Sühne* (Beyond Guilt and Atonement). Its subtitle— 'Attempts to Overcome the Past by One who was Overcome by It'—could equally well be a subtitle for the letters of the young Hamesh, who is faced with the inescapability of exile and to whom the future 'seems like a fearful labyrinth where there's no way out'. However much he is attracted to Bachmann's loneliness, he knows that the loneliness he was 'forced' into has a different origin and will take him 'somewhere else' (2, p. 26). Even his attachment to the beautiful home of the 'dear people' whom he found in Carinthia and who not long before had been members of the Nazi Party,[24] show his immense desire to be accepted in a different Austria. He experienced the pull of home that Améry described so intensely in his essay on the 'homesickness' of those who fled Austria: a person who has had his homeland taken away, wrote Améry, needs 'more' home than 'a whole world of those who have never lost their homeland' can imagine.[25]

When, at the beginning of July 1946, Hamesh set off from Carinthia for Naples before embarking for Palestine, the trauma of the previous loss of his homeland was repeated. The days of the journey were the 'most painful I have ever spent'; his longing for those he had left behind, above all for her whom he loved, was so great that he 'didn't talk to anyone on the whole journey' (5, p. 32). In his first letter from Palestine, he describes the self-destructive homesickness that leaves him feeling 'completely uprooted with nothing to hold on to' as a 'disaster' in which he feels 'as alone as I've never been before' (6, p. 36).

The one thing he didn't hear from her and the 'one thing that still hurts' was that she 'didn't say a single word about seeing each other again or about staying or about meeting again somewhere some day' (6, p. 37). In the letters that follow, he tries to come to terms with the separation, to get away from his own pain and he finds comfort in comforting her as she struggles with the difficulties of post-war Vienna (8, pp. 40–9). In that letter, he also asks a question that is beginning to concern him: How did the people see him then, what was their opinion of him? Did they respect *him* (he doubts that) or 'the power' represented by his victor's uniform (8, p. 45)? This uncertainty is also linked to the fact that he, a foreigner and an alien in the land of his childhood, can no longer interpret their signs and gestures, their language and its disguises with any certainty. There is also an element of fear that he has once more been the victim of a delusion, has once more trusted a 'dream world' which then collapsed (8, p. 46). And he wonders whether in his relationship with Bachmann he has 'been living in illusions again', for she wrote in her letter that she felt 'as if all the bridges' behind her 'have collapsed'. For him, their 'life together' was something exemplary, 'proof that despite everything that has overtaken our two peoples there is still a way—the way of love and understanding' (8, p. 48).

In Hamesh's last letter (11, pp. 55–66), his longest, he reports on developments in Jewish Palestine. This letter sketches—in lively but considered terms—the new society of which he sees himself as part and to the construction of which he is contributing; it is a concrete picture, focusing on everyday life but with a keen eye for the historical and political dimension of the emergent state.[26] For him, being part of the future of Palestine, of a society where Jews can live without persecution, is the best therapy for a past which will not go away, since: 'A person has to live' (11, p. 59).

It is this last letter which looks forward to the future of Palestine but which also gives the most sober description of the impossibility of coming to terms with the collapse of all security, with the experience of 1938, when a child had to wander round the world alone 'just because he had been born a Jew', and whose parents were murdered 'in some gas chamber' and none of whose friends in Palestine, 'mostly from Vienna', 'can enjoy life any more, we try to forget, immerse ourselves in silence and thus bury ourselves all the more in the past we can't forget' (11, p. 58).

The Imaginative Space in the 'Galicia' Chapter of
Das Buch Franza

Anyone familiar with Bachmann's diary and
Hamesh's letters will proceed to read the 'Galicia'
chapter in *Das Buch Franza* differently. Not because
it allows one to decipher it in biographical terms
but because the story of Hamesh sets off a process
of reflection that is not satisfied with the literary
myth of the English officer Lord Percival Glyde in
the novel. Analyzing the forms, the selection
and combination of signs in the construction of
literary characters and regarding the fictional
construct as only one among many possibilities
does not nullify the literary fiction nor does it bind
literature to reality. Another possibility that
suggests itself in the 'Galicia' chapter is the story
of the insignificant soldier—in comparison with
which the literary lustre of Lord Percival Glyde is
forced to pale. The fictional figure of the tall, lean,
Oxford-educated aristocratic British Army officer
is, in all aspects, the opposite of the real Hamesh.
The relationship mentioned in the diary between
Liesl, the prospective doctor, and the English soldier Bob, 'immensely lean and tall', 'very rich and

went to Oxford' and, for the writer of the diary, 'quite unapproachable' (p. 13), is turned into the construct of Franza's love for Lord Percival Glyde— an all-too elegant literary construct when read in the light of the diary and the letters. The real story of Jack Hamesh would perhaps also have been the 'more real' solution in literary terms, for the fact that the memory of him was in the writer's mind is evident in phrases such as 'the loveliest spring' and 'the loveliest summer' taken over from the war diary, and in the conscious transfer of her own story to another relationship mentioned in the diary.[27] Hamesh remains an imaginative space in the novel; Lord Percival Glyde his precise antithesis, a person who listened 'condescendingly',[28] who 'didn't keep in touch' and 'didn't want her address'.[29]

Was it such constructs that caused Bachmann to regard the largely completed novel as a failure? 'It's not only the poor passages and some pages that bother me,' she wrote on 20 November 1965 to her publisher Klaus Piper, 'the manuscript strikes me as a hopeless allusion to something that hasn't yet been written.' She would, she said, 'rewrite the book because of that.' She did not do so but it is revealing that, as the editors of *Todesarten* note, this intention marks the transition to the *Todesarten* projects on Fanny Goldmann and Malina.[30]

Hans Höller
February 2010

Notes

1   In southern Austria; the offices were in the Kaiser von Österreich hotel in Hermagor.

2   Jean Améry, *Ressentiments* in Jean Amery, *Werke*, VOL. 2: *Jenseits von Schuld und Sühne/Unmeisterliche Wanderungen/Örtlichkeiten* (Gerhard Scheit ed.) (Stuttgart, 2002), p. 131 (=Jean Amery, *Werke*, Irene Heidelberger-Leonard ed.).

3   See Jack Hamesh, Letter 2, pp. 24–27. The homeless refugee's longing for a friendly home is noticeable in many of his letters. In Letter 8, pp. 40–49, he explains why this longing is so important to him, him of all people: 'Me especially! For I lacked what other people possessed their whole life through without appreciating it.'

4   Part of Vellach; not to be confused with Obervellach in the Möll Valley, also in Carinthia.

5   German and Slovene.

6   In the afterword to the new edition of his novel *Unvollendete Symphonie* (Unfinished Symphony, 1952), praised as a *roman à clef* about Bachmann, Hans Weigel regarded the story of the books—Bachmann's 'desperate search for banned books during the war in Klagenfurt'—as one of the many things that makes biographical 'sense' (see Hans Weigel, *Unvollendete Symphonie,* Graz/Vienna/Cologne, 1992, p. 197).

7   P. 14. In German, the type of apple tree is a *Wallischbaum*, which etymologically contains the word *walsch* or 'southern', 'Romance'—'Italian'. The Italian border is only about 10 km to the south of the Gail valley, the centre of which is Hermagor.

8   Paul Celan, letter to Ingeborg Bachmann, 31 October 1953 (Letter 35 in *Herzzeit*). See Ingeborg Bachmann, Paul Celan, *Briefwechsel* (Bertrand Badiou, Hans Höller, Andrea Stoll and Barbara Wiedemann eds) (Frankfurt, 2008), p. 64.

9   *Gau*: a territorial unit of the Nazi Party.

10 In the post-war denazification process, 'follower' (*Mitläufer*) designated the lowest category of involvement in Nazi activities.

11 Ingeborg Bachmann, *Drei Wege zum See* in Ingeborg Bachmann, '*Todesarten*'-Projekt, VOL. 4: *Der 'Simultan'-Band und andere späte Erzählungen* (Monika Albrecht and Dirk Göttsche eds) (Munich/Zurich, 1995), p. 361 (= Ingeborg Bachmann, '*Todesarten*'-Projekt. *Kritische Ausgabe*, Monika Albrecht and Dirk Göttsche eds, under the direction of Robert Pichl).

12 Ingeborg Bachmann, *Malina. Roman* in Ingeborg Bachmann, '*Todesarten*'-Projekt, VOL. 3.1: *Malina* (Dirk Göttsche ed., with Monika Albrecht), p. 50f.

13 Ibid., p. 503. In an interview with Ilse Haim after *Malina* was published the author said, 'the things that happened between her eighteenth and twenty-fith year, the destruction of herself as a person, have been transferred to the dreams' (Ingeborg Bachmann, *Wir müssen wahre Sätze finden. Gespräche und Interviews*, Christine Koschel and Inge von Seidenbaum eds, Munich/Zurich, 1983, p. 108 [trans. MM]).

14 Interview with Toni Kirchlechner, 9 April 1971, in ibid., p. 97.

15 Ingeborg Bachmann, *der Tod wird kommen* in
    Ingeborg Bachmann, *Werke,* VOL. 2 (Christine
    Koschel, Inge von Weidenbaum, Clemens
    Münster eds) (Munich/Zurich, 1978), p. 275.

16 Ingeborg Bachmann, 'Politik und Physis' in
    Ingeborg Bachmann, *Kritische Schriften*
    (Monika Albrecht and Dirk Göttsche eds)
    (Munich/Zurich, 2005), p. 373f.

17 Ingeborg Bachmann, '*Der Zug war pünktlich
    (über Heinrich Böll)*' in Bachmann, *Kritische
    Schriften,* p. 13, p. 373f.

18 Ingeborg Bachmann, 'Frankfurter Vorlesun-
    gen' in ibid., p. 299.

19 Ingeborg Bachmann, 'Music und Dichtung'
    in ibid., p. 251.

20 Ingeborg Bachmann, 'Ausfahrt' (Setting
    Out) in Bachmann, *Werke,* p. 29.

21 See letter 6, pp. 35–38. She told her parents
    about the—for Jack Hamesh—surprise visit
    in a letter (Graz 15. 6. 1946, in Bachmann's
    private papers, Kötschach/Carinthia): 'I'll
    probably come home in the evening on 22.
    VI for several important reasons . . . But
    don't tell Jack, not that I'm coming, nor any-
    thing else' (trans. MM).

22 See the discussion about the 'exemplary
    nature' of her relationship with Paul Celan

in Bachmann, Celan, *Herzzeit. Der Briefwechsel*, p. 25f.

23 Ingeborg Bachmann tells the story of this food parcel in a letter to her parents (19 April 1947, Bachmann's private papers, Kötschach).

24 The fathers of the families Jack Hamesh mentions with such gratitude, Dr Herbert Pirker and the dentist Hubert Erber, were both members of the Nazi Party.

25 Jean Améry, *'Wieviel Heimat braucht der Mensch?'* in Jean Amery, *Werke*, VOL. 2: *Jenseits von Schuld und Sühne/Unmeisterliche Wanderjahre/Örtlichkeiten* (Gerhard Scheit ed.) (Stuttgart, 2000), p. 131.

26 See Anne Betten and Miryam Du-nour (eds), *Wir sind die letzten. Fragt uns aus. Gespräche mit den Emigranten der dreißiger Jahre in Israel* (Gerlingen, 1995).

27 'She left it at hints. She said, this isn't the loveliest spring, it's the second loveliest. He gave her a suspicious look, but then she dropped spring one and spring two, and they started to study the names on the gravestones' (Bachmann, *Das Buch Franza*, VOL. 2, p. 169; [trans. MM]).

28 Ibid., p. 181.

29 Ibid., p. 186.
30 Ibid., p. 397.

INGEBORG BACHMANN'S DIARY

The Manuscript

Ingeborg Bachmann's diary from the last months of the war and the period of liberation by the British Army has survived as a typewritten manuscript. The six closely written A4 sheets are in the private archive of her brother and sister. The manuscript is in two parts, each divided into paragraphs. The first part (sheets 1–3) describes the last months of the war and Nazi rule in Klagenfurt. It ends with the sentence: 'No, there's no point in talking to grown-ups any more.' The second part (sheets 4–6) begins on a new page. It documents the liberation of Hermagor and Obervellach and, above all, the meeting with Jack Hamesh.

The manuscript, largely free from typing errors, is presumably a copy—perhaps an extract?—from probably handwritten diary entries, which have not been preserved. That is suggested both by the lack of corrections and the reference to an existing diary in the first sentence: 'Dear Diary.' Also, the at-times-considerable interval between the individual entries and the superimposed structure indicate a revised, abridged fair copy. The war diary was displayed in the exhibition *Ingeborg Bachmann. Schreiben gegen den Krieg/Ingeborg Bachmann. Writing against War* and a lengthy extract printed alongside the English translation in the exhibition catalogue (Hans Höller, Helga Pöcheim and Karl Solibakke eds, Vienna, 2008, pp. 34–49.)

Dating and Topographical Details

The beginning of the diary entries can be dated from the time Bachmann began at the teacher-training college—September 1944—and therefore avoided the danger of having to go 'to Poland'. In the second paragraph, she mentions that the Russians were in Vienna, that is, that the military liberation of Vienna by the Red Army—the middle of March 1945—was already under way. The next paragraph: 'Yesterday the biggest formation we've ever had came' must then refer to the bombing of Klagenfurt on 15 March 1945. It was on that day, as previously on 16 January, that the heaviest Allied air-raids hit Klagenfurt. The following paragraphs deal with the way in which the Nazi officials terrorized the civilian population during the defence of Klagenfurt and the forms of passive resistance put up by a group of young women friends, including Bachmann. The last paragraph contains her preparations for her flight to the Gail valley where her father had a small house, which they usually only occupied during the holidays, in Obervellach (part of Vellach, a district of Hermagor).

The second part starts after the liberation by the troops of the British 8th Army (8 May 1945) as they advanced from Italy over the Plöcken Pass into the Gail valley. After a comment on administrative measures ordered by the military authorities, she mentions the FSS, the Field Security Section, to which Jack Hamesh belonged. Her encounter with him is the main subject of the second part of the diary, which also has the only two dates in the whole typescript: 11 and 14 June.

The Printed Text

The diary is reproduced here in precisely the same order of the paragraphs as in the typescript.

Obvious typing errors have been corrected without comment, omitted words added in square brackets [omitted in the translation—Trans.]. We have retained the double 's', since her typewriter clearly did not have an 'ß'. The spelling of the name 'Dr Hasler' or 'Hasler' was retained although the person concerned is presumably Dr Bernhard Haßler (1892–1969), who taught educational theory and methods at the teacher-training college and was an acquaintance of Matthias Bachmann, Ingeborg's father. The spelling of the French quotation from Baudelaire's *Fleurs du Mal* was not corrected.

Some names which occur in rumours reported in the diary have been indicated solely with initials in line with the right to privacy.

Dating and Description of the Letters

The 11 letters from Jack Hamesh, which are preserved in the Bachmann family's archive of private
papers, run from Easter 1946 to summer 1947.
Since there was no one in the house in Obervellach,
the first letter was left there immediately before
Easter (in 1946, Easter Sunday fell on 21 April). The
last—last preserved?—letter is dated 16 July 1947
and was posted in Tel Aviv. Letters 1–7 are handwritten, the last three from Tel Aviv typed; NO. 4
and NO. 10 are telegrams. The first typewritten
letter has many handwritten additions and corrections. Even in the last letter, Hamesh is still apolo-
gizing for not writing by hand. When Hamesh
wrote the first letter, he was about 26. He had probably hardly written any German for eight years.

The envelopes are very informative since they
give Bachmann's changing addresses—she spent the

summer semester of 1946 at the University of Graz before moving to Vienna University in the winter semester of 1947/48—and the various places from which they were sent: Hermagor, Villach Release Camp, Naples and his two addresses in Tel Aviv. Listed below are the place and date of the postmark and of the stamps of the postal censor's office as well as any traces of the letter having been opened by the British Military Administration (abolished by a resolution of the Allied Council of 14 August 1953):

1. Handwritten, envelope missing. The letter will have been put in with the presents. Probably 19 or 20 April 1946 (Easter Sunday was on 21 April).

2. Handwritten letter to 'INGE BACHMANN / GRAZ, BROCKMANNGASSE 35a / (c/o Hofler)'. Postmark: Hermagor, 17.6.46. Stamp of the civilian censor's office in the British Zone. From 'J. Hamesh/Hermagor'.

3. Handwritten letter to 'Fr. Inge Bachmann / Ober Vellach 22 / Gailtal in / Kärnten / Österreich'. Postmark: Seebach bei Villach 28.6.46 and Hermagor 1.7.46.

4 Telegram to Ingeborg Bachmann / Obervellach Gailtal / Austria, Napoli 3.7.[1946], 16.40, and Obervellach, 4.7.46, 17.10 [in 1946 the telegram forms of Obervellach post office were still headed 'Deutsche Reichspost'].

5 Handwritten letter to 'Frl. Ingeborg Bach-mann / Ober-Vellach / Gailtal / <u>Kärnten—Österreich</u>'. From 'J. Hamesh'. Postmark: Graz 3.[?]7.46 [the letter, with an Austrian postage stamp on the reverse could possibly have been brought from Naples to Graz by an acquaintance and posted there]. The month on the letterhead should be corrected to July 1946.

6 Handwritten airmail letter to 'Frl. / Inge-borg Bachmann / Obervellach 21 / Gailtal / Kärnten / Austria'. Postage stamp torn off. Stamp of the civilian censor's office in the British Zone. From 'J. Hamesh c/o Arseh Steiner / Tel-Aviv, Hara Kewethstr. 4 / <u>Palestine</u>'. Postmark: Hermagor, 6.8.46. The letter was opened by the censors and stuck back again with a strip of paper.

7 Handwritten sheet of notepaper, folded in two; stiff paper. Given the fold, the size of the sheet and the colour of the ink, it could have been enclosed with Letter 6.

8 Typewritten airmail letter with hand-written additions and corrections to 'Frl. Ingeborg Bachmann / Wien III., / Beatrix-gasse 26 / I / bei Winkler / Austria'. Postage stamp torn off. Stamp of the Austrian censor's office. From 'J. Hamesh c/o Steiner / Tel-Aviv, Hara Kewethstr. 4. / <u>Palestine</u>'. Stamp: Registered 3.11.46. Postmark: Vienna 16.11.46. The letter was opened by the censors.

9 Typewritten airmail letter [with Christmas greetings printed on the back] to 'Frl. Ingeborg Bachmann / Ober-Vellach Gailtal / Kärnten / AUSTRIA'. From 'J. Hamesh c/o Steiner / Hara Kewethstr. 4 Tel-Aviv / PALESTINE'. Postmark: Hermagor 31.12.[?]46.

10 Telegram to Inge Bachmann / Obervellach 21 / Gailtal Ktn. Austria. From: Tel-Aviv, 23.6.1957, 12.15, and Villach, 15.35.

11 Typewritten airmail letter with handwritten corrections and postscript to 'Frl.
Ingeborg Bachmann / Ober-Vellach 21 /
Gailtal / Kärnten / AUSTRIA'. Postage
stamp torn off. Stamp of the civilian
censor's office of the British Zone. From
'J. Hamesh Y. Nagarastr. 6 Tel-Aviv'.

*Particular Characteristics of Hamesh's German
and its Reproduction in the Text*

The grammar and spelling of the letters has been
retained. The purpose of this retention is to docu-
ment the story of a Jew who was cast out of the
German language—to be precise, out of Austrian
German—to whom his mother tongue is no longer
a matter of course. His letters contain peculiarities
of Viennese spoken German: for example, the frequent use of the accusative instead of the dative.

In the handwritten letters the frequent lack of
punctuation, especially the sparse use of the
comma, is often offset by varying distances between
words and different indents at the beginning of
paragraphs. These nuances in the gaps between
words could not be reproduced in the printed text;

in the case of paragraph indents, only striking differences were retained.

The attempt to stick as closely as possible to the original form of the text is not only for documentary purposes but also derives from our desire to accord the writing of a largely unknown young man who was driven out of the German language the same care and attention as the texts of important writers. It is a matter of great regret to us that we have so far been unable to find any trace of him. The name Hamesh is completely unfamiliar in Israel. Perhaps this publication will help find out more about the life of Jack Hamesh.

It was impossible to reproduce most of the spelling and grammatical errors, and to introduce 'equivalent' mistakes seemed to me to go against the editor's desire to retain the authenticity of the original. I initially wondered about reproducing Hamesh's 'sparse' use of punctuation but eventually decided that the interests of both the writer and the reader would be best served by normalizing the language in the English version.

Mike Mitchell

My comments on Jack Hamesh's [Hamesch] letters in the first edition of the *War Diary* concluded with: 'Perhaps this publication will help find out more about the life of Jack Hamesh.' The publication of his letters did indeed help to give a name to the man Ingeborg Bachmann knew as Jack Hamesch and a life-history going beyond the letters. His story is reflected in the transformation of his name from Jakob Marasch to Jakob Chamicz in Vienna, to Jack Hamesch in the British Army and to Yaakov Chamish, his name in Israel.

I had started my research in the summer of 2009 with Wolf-Erich Eckstein of the Registry of the Vienna Jewish Community. Neither the name Hamesch nor what I assumed would be the German or Yiddish variant of Fünfer/Finfer were recorded in the registers or in the lists of *kindertransports* from Vienna to England. There were no entries worth pursuing under that name in the Vienna

City and State Archives either and my request to be allowed to go through all births registered with the first name Jakob was rejected for reasons of data protection.

When the archive of the Jewish Community received more and more enquiries following the publication of Bachmann's war diary and Hamesch's letters, and Frau Dr Eva Irblich, a retired official from the Austrian National Library, took up the search with great energy, making it a personal crusade, Wolf-Erich Eckstein spent one weekend studying the documented history of all those children born in 1920 with the name Jakob—and he managed to find a clue to the man we were look- ing for.

He was able to establish a connection between Jakob Marasch, a member of the Community born 16 March 1920 in the Brigittenau hospital (Vienna XX), and Jack Hamesch. In an entry of 26 March 1931, the name Jakob Marasch is noted as: 'cor- rectly Chamicz'. (In the registration documents of the Vienna City and State Archive, the forms Chamisch and Chaimicz also occur.) His mother, born 26 February 1890, appears, in an entry crossed out in 1925, as Heni Marasch, unskilled, place of

origin Szczurowice, Brody district in what was at
that time the region of Galicia, now part of Ukraine;
his father, Abraham Marasch, died in 1922. In a
later entry from 1925, his mother is noted under
the name Heni Chamicz and as 'single'—which was
due to the fact that the ritual marriage was never
officially registered.

Jakob Marasch was not put on the official
Viennese registry until 5 October 1926, with his
address given as the orphanage of the Jewish
Community, 2 Probusgasse, Vienna XIX. Being in
service as a home help, his mother would have
been unable to look after and bring up her child
herself. She died of tuberculosis on 26 December
1936. The last entry concerning Jakob Chamicz is:
'emigrated 1. 11. 1938 to Palestine'.

The Austrian State Archives in Vienna pos-
sesses a claim for restitution payment by Jakob
Chamisch (Jacob Chamish) from 1964 which gives
his first address as 'hostel for infants in Neuleng-
bach' and his last one before emigration as the
Jewish Community Apprentices' Hostel in the 9th
district of Vienna, 26 Grünetorgasse. The restitution documentation reveals that Jakob Chamisch
started to train as a cobbler in 1934. After 7 January

1938, he would have been eligible to take the examination to become a journeyman but that was no longer possible after the entry of Hitler's troops on 13 March of that year. Since he never obtained Austrian nationality, he remained 'stateless' in Austria.

In the British Protectorate of Palestine, to which he emigrated in November 1938, he worked in several kibbutzim as an agricultural labourer until 1941; from June 1941 to the summer of 1946, he was a soldier in the British Army and stationed in Hermagor from May 1945 to June 1946 as an interpreter. After his discharge from the army in Palestine, he lived in Tel Aviv from 1946 to 1965. He married for the first time in 1949. He first worked as a docker and from 1952, after injuring his arm, in the Jaffa harbour administration. In 1965, he moved to Ashdod. He died on 21 July 1987, at the age of sixty-seven, in the course of a heart operation in Tel Hashomer Hospital in Ramat Gan. There are two sons from his two marriages. Today the son from his first marriage is living in the USA, the one from his second marriage in Israel.

Eva Irblich has made contact with both sons and now they are on friendly terms with Heinz

Bachmann, Ingeborg Bachmann's brother. They knew hardly anything about their father's early life and his meeting with Ingeborg Bachmann. All that was left of it was a signed photo of her in their father's effects. It is dated the day of Hamesch's departure from Hermagor, 23 June 1946. Heinz Bachmann certified the photo during a visit to the younger son in Israel in October 2010.

Like many survivors of the Shoah, Hamesch told his children very little about his past. When they were themselves already over sixty, his sons suddenly found themselves confronted with a part of their father's life-story that was almost entirely unknown to them.

When I expressed my misgivings about making the letters of a man who has gone missing publicly available, Wolf-Erich Eckstein just smiled and said, 'What do you expect, without the book no one would ever have bothered about the man's story?'

Hans Höller